Pebble® Plus

CARS, CARS, CARS

T0100912

OLD CARS

by Melissa Abramovitz

Gail Saunders-Smith, PhD, Consulting Editor

Consultant: Leslie Mark Kendall, Curator
Petersen Automotive Museum
Los Angeles, California

CAPSTONE PRESS
a capstone imprint

Pebble Plus is published by Capstone Press,
1710 Roe Crest Drive, North Mankato, Minnesota 56003.
www.capstonepub.com

Library of Congress Cataloging-in-Publication Data
Abramovitz, Melissa, 1954–
  Old cars / by Melissa Abramovitz.
      p. cm.—(Pebble plus. Cars, cars, cars)
  Includes bibliographical references and index.
  Summary: "Simple text and color photographs describe nine old cars"—Provided by the publisher.
  Audience: K-3.
  ISBN 978-1-62065-090-5 (library binding)
  ISBN 978-1-62065-875-8 (paperback)
  ISBN 978-1-4765-1075-0 (eBook PDF)
  1. Antique and classic cars—United States—Juvenile literature. 2. Automobiles—United States—History—Juvenile literature. I. Title. II. Series: Pebble plus. Cars, cars, cars.
  TL23.A23 2013
  629.222—dc23   2012031832

Editorial Credits
Erika L. Shores, editor; Kyle Grenz, designer; Laura Manthe, production specialist

Photo Credits
Alamy: Shawshots, 5, The Reading Room, 17, World History Archive, 19; Dreamstime: Margojh, cover (middle), Mastroraf, 21; Getty Images: Bettmann, 7, George Eastman House/Nathan Lazarnick, 11, Historical, 15; James P. Rowan: 13; Shutterstock: 1xpert, cover (background), David Huntley, cover (right); Wikimedia: Autoworldmobilia/Public Domain, 9, Thesupermat/cropped/CC Attribution-Share Alike 3.0 Unported, cover (left)

Artistic Effects
Shutterstock: 1xpert

Note to Parents and Teachers

The Cars, Cars, Cars set supports national science standards related to science, technology, and society. This book describes and illustrates old cars. The images support early readers in understanding the text. The repetition of words and phrases helps early readers learn new words. This book also introduces early readers to subject-specific vocabulary words, which are defined in the Glossary section. Early readers may need assistance to read some words and to use the Table of Contents, Glossary, Read More, Internet Sites, and Index sections of the book.

Printed in the United States   5519

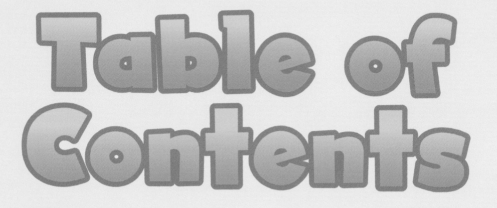

Table of Contents

Old

Before cars, people used horses

or trains to travel. Cars let

people travel farther and faster.

What were the first cars like?

Big Duesenberg Model Js sold

for up to $20,000.

That would be like paying

more than $300,000 today.

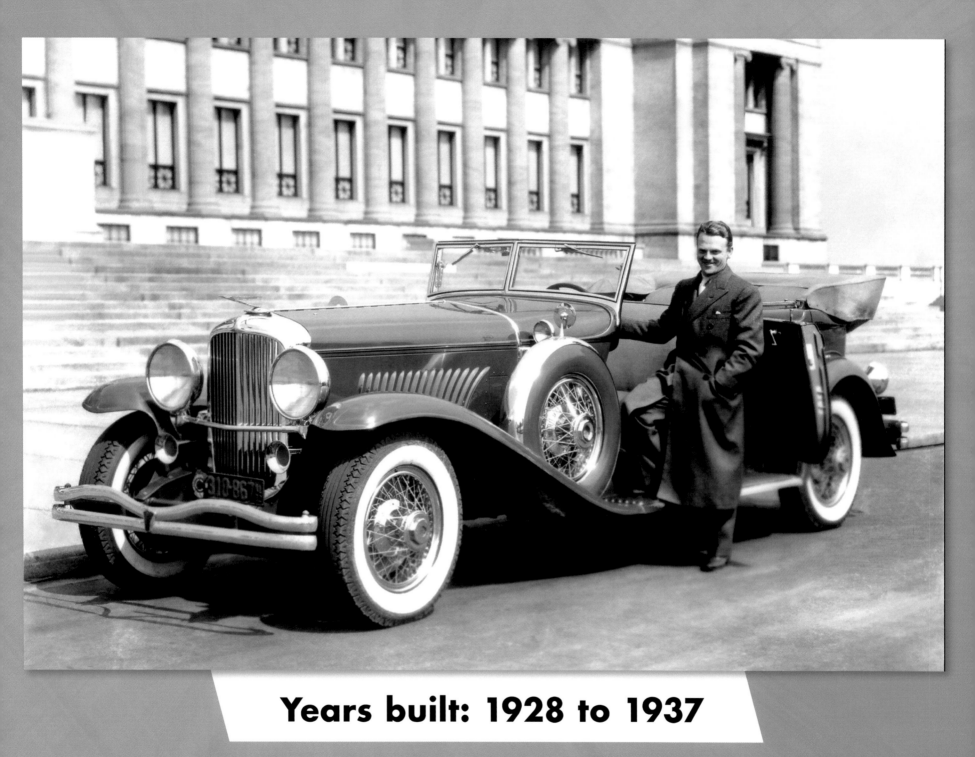

Years built: 1928 to 1937

The Golden Submarine was one of the first race cars with a roof. It was safer and faster than other early racers. It went more than 100 miles (161 kilometers) per hour.

Year built: 1917

A Stutz Bearcat was one

of America's first sports cars.

It had no doors or roof

and only a tiny round windshield.

Years built: 1912 to 1915

Older

The OctoAuto had eight wheels.
All those wheels made the ride
less bumpy. But eight-wheelers
never became popular.

Year built: 1911

Before the Ford Model T,

only rich people could buy cars.

Factories made 15 million of

these cars that most people

could afford.

Years built: 1908 to 1927

It took 20 minutes to start

a steam-powered Stanley.

But in 1906, a Stanley set

a speed record. It reached

nearly 128 mph (206 kph).

Years built: 1897 to 1924

Oldest

The first electric car in
the United States was built
by William Morrison.
The Electric Buggy's top speed
was less than 20 mph (32 kph).

Year built: 1891

Karl Benz built one of the first vehicles with a gas engine. The Motorwagen had just three wheels.

Year built: 1885

Many people think of Nicolas-Joseph Cugnot's steam-powered vehicle as the world's first car. It moved only 2 mph (3.2 kph).

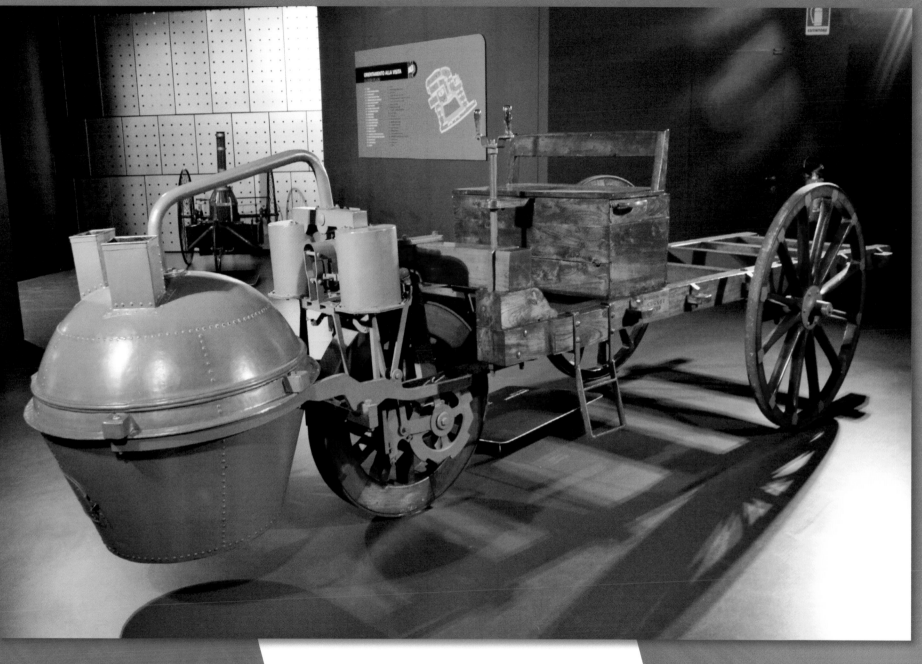

Year built: 1769

Glossary

afford—to have enough money to pay for something

electric—having or using electricity

engine—a machine that makes the power needed to move something

popular—liked or enjoyed by many people

record—when something is done better than anyone has ever done it before

sports car—a car built to reach high speeds

steam—water that has turned into water vapor

windshield—a window on the front part of a vehicle

Read More

Lassieur, Allison. *Cars 100 Years Ago.* Mankato, Minn.: Amicus, 2012.

Oxlade, Chris. *The Car.* Tales of Invention. Chicago: Heinemann Library, 2011.

Raum, Elizabeth. *The History of the Car.* Inventions that Changed the World. Chicago: Heinemann Library, 2008.

Internet Sites

FactHound offers a safe, fun way to find Internet sites related to this book. All of the sites on FactHound have been researched by our staff.

Here's all you do:

Visit *www.facthound.com*

Type in this code: 9781620650909095

Check out projects, games and lots more at
www.capstonekids.com

Index

Word Count: 223
Grade: 1
Early-Intervention Level: 23